SHROUDED
IN
DARKNESS

Striping Away The Veil To See The Source Of Turmoil

LARRY ADAMS

I0178140

ISBN: 978-0-9893460-4-7

Table of Contents

Other books by Larry Adams
Deception In Gospel Presentation
How Does God Express His Sovereignty?
Six Biblical Issues Against "God Is In Control"
Discipling A New Believer
Revelation: A Fresh Perspective

Preface

John 3:19-21 (NASB) *"19 This is the judgment, that the Light has come into the world, and men loved the darkness rather than the Light, for their deeds were evil. 20 For everyone who does evil hates the Light, and does not come to the Light for fear that his deeds will be exposed. 21 But he who practices the truth comes to the Light, so that his deeds may be manifested as having been wrought in God."*

Ephesians 6:12 (NASB) *"12 For our struggle is not against flesh and blood, but against the rulers, against the powers, against the world forces of this darkness, against the spiritual forces of wickedness in the heavenly places."*

Light versus darkness. Good versus evil. Sin versus righteousness. Peace versus turmoil. These, and others, are all labels for the spiritual warfare everyone in the world is involved in — whether they know it or not. The evil entities do their deeds in darkness, which they are the masters over. All truly born again Christians should be aware of this warfare, but, sadly, very few of them are aware. In these verses of Scripture, John is using light and dark as analogies for good and evil, truth and evil. John is describing the battle we are all part of as being either in darkness performing evil, or in Light performing what is righteous and truthful. Paul identifies the real forces that operate within darkness, the spiritual powers and forces in the heavenlies. In this discussion the words light, good, and righteousness will be used to indicate the things which are Godly, while dark, darkness, evil, and sin will be used to represent the things of Satan.

Revelation 12:9 and 20:2 gives us four names for the evil one: dragon, serpent of old, devil, and Satan. These names will be used interchangeably throughout the discussion, along with other names used in the Bible for the evil one. There are at least 24 names for the evil one throughout Scripture. In Genesis chapters 1 and 2, we find God setting the stage for the ultimate spiritual war. Genesis chapter 3 introduces the adversary, the serpent, and the first spiritual battle which Eve and Adam lost. Revelation gives us a picture of how the war is going to end. (Spoiler Alert: God wins!) In between the beginning and end are many skirmishes, descriptions of what God requires to be on the winning side, and many examples of the tactics of the adversary.

Sigmund Freud battled depression most of his life, and just as he failed to believe in a living, viable , active God, he mentioned "devil" in many of his letters, but failed to believe that the devil was an active adversary. His ideas about evil and the devil are, "obscure, unfeeling and unloving powers determin[ing] men's fate." He almost believed, but not quite, just like most people today. God inspired the written Bible, and it contains over 170 references to Satan, his methods, purpose, and results, and his origin and demise. God apparently believes in the existence of Satan as an active entity, and has taken the effort to inform us of him in detail.

Some deceived people who believe the Bible and believe in God think that we should not mention anything about this evil entity because it "gives him too much glory." When one considers how much God has stated about Satan, the comment of these deceived people amounts to an insult of God. The approach of the following discussion will only focus on what and how God has said and described about Satan without embellishment. I seriously doubt that God would give Satan too much "glory" and if we stay within the parameters that God has provided, we won't be giving him any "glory" either. T;he 'excuse' of giving glory to the evil one is simply another of Satan's deceptions to help him work in darkness.

Shrouded In Darkness

There are several points that need to be clarified, foundational points that will enable us to understand how and why things are the way they are on both sides of the spiritual war we are in. We need to understand the behaviors that are inherent to both sides of the issue; that there are only two sides to the issues, the goals of each side, the end results or outcomes of the behaviors of each side. With that information we can evaluate situational process and end results and work back to which side initiated the situation. We will find that determining which source is to blame becomes very simple and uncomplicated. One of the keys to victory is understanding the tactics and outcomes or goals of your enemy.

Not everyone has a spiritual world view such that they believe in God or anything spiritual. Just because someone might not believe in gravity, does not mean they will float off earth's surface into space - gravity works even if you don't believe in it. Science has replaced some people's world view, but, science is concerned with physical observation and measurement and cannot observe or measure anything spiritual. Science cannot prove or disprove that anything spiritual exists. It is possible that we are influenced by things we know nothing about.

Permit me to emphasize that Satan is in no way anywhere equal to God. As a created being, Satan will always be inferior to God, and always an enemy of God and all mankind that God created in His own image and likeness. One of Satan's desires is to replace God, however, IF that could happen, Satan would annihilate himself because he would eliminate the source and power that keeps him a viable entity - Colossians 1:17.

Satan is literally getting away with murder because he has blinded the eyes of the people of the world (2 Corinthians 4:4), effectively working while shrouded in darkness. Let's shed some light into that darkness.

Shrouded In Darkness

Defining the Context

The old adage goes: "Context is everything." When the context is <u>not</u> taken into account, the meanings of things and conclusions are all skewed and no longer represent the truth. Truth and context go hand-in-hand, they are inseparable. The Bible presents us with the context of itself in the first three chapters. Simply stated, God sets up the environment for a war and introduces the adversary in the war.

Details of the top commander of each side are introduced throughout the rest of the Bible. These top commanders are part of the overall context of the war. Some philosophies either do not believe that God exists, or Satan the adversary does not exist, and some do not believe either exist. The perspective of this discussion is that both exist. If information regarding other philosophies is desired, I would suggest starting with a very well written book by Richard E. Simmons III, *"Reflection on the existence of God."* And then consider that God exists and He is the one who inspired and has preserved the written Bible and it does include the adversary in the first skirmish of the war. If Satan doesn't exist, and God inspired the written record, then God is a liar and no one has any hope of anything (assuming that somehow people, Earth, galaxies, etc., somehow overcame the enormous odds against their existence and somehow did come into existence).

Identifying the enemy

So, let's start with the question: "Who is the adversary?" The Bible's descriptions of Satan will be presented here. And if you are interested, the Christians Godly characteristics and God's provision to overcome the enemy are listed in Appendix A *"What the Believer needs to overcome to be what God intended."* Isaiah 14 and Ezekiel 28 provide us with the most coherent description of his origins. Basically, "pride of self" persuaded this being to desire to replace God with himself, to assume a position equal to or greater than his creator. Other references related to his origin can be found in 1 Chronicles 21:1; Psalms 48:1, 68:15; Isaiah 2:2. Please take the time and read these reference passages so you can verify what is being discussed about our enemy.

His kingdom is the earth and air, Ephesians 2:2, 6:12; 1 Peter 5:8-9. He still has access to the heavenly throne, Job 1:6; Revelation 12:10. His head was bruised by Christ (defeated) as prophesied by God in Genesis 3:15. He is going to receive judgment for his sin of pride, John 12:31, 16:11; Colossians 2:13-15. God's grace for man's salvation holds off his final demise, John 3:18; Revelation 5:18-19. His judgment will really happen, 1 Corinthians 15:25; Psalms 2:9; Revelation 2:27, 12:5. He will be cast out of heaven, down to earth shortly before his final judgment, Revelation 12: 7-12. His end will be the Lake of Fire, Revelation 20:10

Satan was created by God, not made equal to God, Proverbs 16:4. He defies and despises God and truth, John 8:44. He was given limited power, Job 1:8-12. He commands a hierarchy of demons (many understand these to be fallen angels, those who also despise God and reject truth), Ephesians 6:10-12. He is capable of masquerading as an "angel of light", 2 Corinthians 11:14-15. He only desires to steal, kill and destroy, John 10:10; Job 1:6-2:7. He rules people who are outside of God's protection, the people of the world, Ephesians 2:1-3; Luke 22:25. Believers can stray after Satan, 1 Timothy 5:15.

He keeps seeking an opportune time to tempt us, causing us to sin, Luke 4:13; 1 John 3:8. He tries to hide the actual truth about God, 2 Corinthians 4:3-4. He offers counterfeit promises he can't fulfill, Genesis 3:4-5. He twists God's words to fit his own purposes, Genesis 3:1-5. He is a liar and the father of lies, John 8:44. He oppresses people (exercises power over), Acts 10:38; a woman had been bound (to tie or bind) for 18 years, Luke 13:16. Paul's thorn in the flesh was a messenger of Satan, 2 Corinthians 12:7. Satan currently has the power of death and suffering and disease, Hebrews 2:14.

Satan is referenced by several names throughout Scripture. They are:

Lucifer ('star of the morning', shining one), Isaiah 14:12. Satan, Mark 4:15 (adversary, enemy). Devil, Matthew 4:1-11 (slanderer, one who makes a false malicious statement, typically injurious to one's reputation). Prince of the power of the air, Ephesians 2:2 (this refers to his domination of worldly human subjects). The god of this age, 2 Corinthians 4:4 (this is a reference to his rule over the present darkness of the world). King of death, Hebrews 2:14 (a reference to his power of death). Prince of this world, John 12:31 (refers to his current rulership of the world, soon to be deposed at Christ's second coming). Ruler of darkness, Ephesians 6:12 (refers to his current rule, authority and power over the spiritual darkness of the world).

Leviathan, Isaiah 27:1 (a dragon like creature). Dragon, Revelation 12:7ff. Deceiver, Revelation 20:10 (one who lies to trick or deceive). Apollyon, Revelation 9:11 (a destroyer who causes damage beyond use or repair). Beelzebub, Matthew 12:24 (lord of the flies, lord of dung, the dung god). Belial 2 Corinthians 6:15 (the personification of all that is evil). Wicked one, Matthew 13:38 (evil or mischievous by nature). Tempter, 1 Thessalonians 3:5 (provocation to cause one to do wrong). Accuser of the brethren, Revelation 12:10 (to charge or place blame or fault on another).

Angel of light, 2 Corinthians 11:14-15 (one of his deceptive appearances). Liar and father of lies, John 8:44 (to intentionally give false information). Murderer, John 8:44 (to deliberately kill, see Job 1:13-19). Enemy, Matthew 13:39 (hostility and hatred toward God, opposes interests of, and intends to hurt God himself). Roaring lion, 1 Peter 5:8 (destructive threat). Serpent, Genesis 3:4-5. Thief, John 10:10 (one who steals).

Another name that could be used is imitator — this comes from Satan's imitation of God and Godly things as part of his deception. This is detailed as follows:

Tares among wheat, Matthew 13:24-39. Evil trinity as opposed to holy trinity, Revelation 13 & 20:10. Also, he imitates the persons of the trinity: God the Father versus witchcraft, God the Son versus sorcery; God the Holy Spirit versus divination. The son of perdition (destruction) to oppose the Son of God, John 17:12. Tares are from the evil one, the good wheat is from the farmer, Matthew :13:36. The mystery of iniquity (2 Thessalonians 2:7) in opposition to the mystery of Godliness (1 Timothy 3:16). 144,000 sealed by God (Revelation 7:3,14:1) opposed by the Antichrist's mark of the beast (Revelation13:16).

The Spirit searches the deep things of God (1 Corinthians 2:10) opposed by the deep things of Satan (Revelation 2:24). Miracles performed by Christ in the Gospel accounts opposed by Satanic signs and wonders through the false prophet (Revelation 13). Christ on His throne in heaven (Ephesians 1:20) opposed by Satan's throne (Revelation 2:13). The Church versus the synagogue of Satan (Revelation 2:9). Jesus, the light of the world (John 8:12) opposed by Satan appearing as an angel of light (2 Corinthians 11:14).

Sometimes there are direct manifestations of satanic power: Daniel 11; 2 Thessalonians 2; Revelation 13 [future]. Satan's intent is to deceive all people and the whole world, 2 Thessalonians 2:9 Revelation 12:9,

Shrouded In Darkness

20:2-3,7-8. Satanic temptation of our lusts by persuasion result in death, James 1:14-15. Our following sin proceeds from the heart, Mark 7:21-23. Satan wants us to sacrifice to false gods, Deuteronomy 32:17; Leviticus 17:7. We have the choice of Jesus or demons, not both, 1 Corinthians 10:20-21. Some will not repent of the worship of false gods even when faced with the final judgment, Revelation 9:20. Satan hates not only God but those who are truly His, 2 Peter 1:4. Satan does not want God to love the unsaved through believers, Romans 5:5; John 16:33, 17:15; 2 Timothy 3:12; 1 John 3:13; 1 Peter 5:7-9; Ephesians 6:10-12. The end time results of people following satanic temptation will be many, including believers holding to forms of godliness (traditions) but denying God's power, 2 Timothy 3:1-5.

Satan uses demons (fallen angels) to provide false teaching through church members, doctrines of demons, 1 Timothy 4;1-2; 1 Kings 22:21-22; Revelation 2:24; 2 Corinthians 2:10; 2 Peter 2:1.

Jesus states that Satan is a king of a kingdom, Matthew 12:26. Satan is king over the kingdoms of the world system, Matthew 4; Luke 4. Satan's hosts are wicked, unclean, vicious, Matthew 8:28, 10:1, 12:43-45; Mark 5:2-5, 9:20.

The Holy Spirit restrains Satan until He is taken out of the way, 2 Thessalonians 2:7. God puts limits on what Satan can do, Job 1-2. Satan is the prince of the world and this age, John 12:31, 14:30, 16:11; Ephesians 2:2, 6:12; 2 Corinthians 4:4; Luke 4:5-7, 1 John 4:4. Satan's world system is corrupt, 2 Peter 1:4, 2:20; James 1:27; 1 John 4:3, 5:4; John 14:30. Satan has power over physical well-being, Hebrews 2:14; Acts 10:38; Luke 13:16, 22:31-32; Job 1:9-12; 2 Corinthians 12:7. Satan hates believers, 1 John 3:13.

Satan does have a few impotencies and limitations, 1 John 4:4, 3:1, 4:5; 1 Corinthians 2:14-15; 2

5

Corinthians 4:3-4; Romans 3:11. His world and its lusts and works will pass away, 1 John 2:17; 2 Peter 3:10. People can deceive and be deceived [a characteristic of Satan's activity], 2 Timothy 3:13. The unsaved are children of Satan, Matthew 13:38; John 8:44; Acts 13:10; Ephesians 2:2-3; Colossians 3:6. God's wrath will come on the children of disobedience, the unsaved, Ephesians 5:6.

One of Satan's favorite weapons is fear. We understand this mostly by proper inference from statements about God's love, peace and faith conquering or casting out fear. The use of the word "fear" throughout the Bible can have two meanings that need to be determined within the context used in. One meaning is "reverence and respect,": the other is based on horror or terror, which is the more typical meaning of the word "fear." The "fear" used by the devil is the horror and terror version. Some of the verses countering that horror and terror type of fear are: Psalms 23:4, 27:1, 34:4, 56:3; Isaiah 41:10; John 14:27; Romans 8:15; 2 Timothy 1:7; 1 Peter 5:8; 1 John 4:18; Revelation 2:10.

I have listed most of the over 170 references I have collected about Satan in the Bible. If you started this book with the idea that Satan does not exist, and have gotten this far, please, consider that God is truth and cannot lie (Titus 1:2; Numbers 23:19) — so why did God inspire to be written all these references about Satan and preserve them over the several thousand years it has existed? To deny that Satan exists after this evidence is basically to call God a liar — not a good situation to find oneself in.

Please, keep in mind that Satan is a created being, and on that basis alone, is inferior to God, nowhere even close to being on the same par with God. The ending of Isaiah 43:10 states: "...Before Me there was no God formed, and there will be none after Me." There will never be any form of competition or collaboration with the Lord God Almighty Creator of Heaven and Earth. He is the one and only God for eternity.

Identifying the Creator of Heaven and Earth

Jeremiah 9:24 (NASB) *"24 but let him who boasts boast of this, that he understands and knows Me, that I am the Lord who exercises lovingkindness, justice and righteousness on earth; for I delight in these things," declares the Lord."*

Understanding and knowing the Lord provides us access to his character and attributes, some of which are lovingkindness, justice and righteousness (among many more).

Love is the basis for redemption (Deuteronomy 7:7-10, 10:9; 2 Chronicles 9:8; Nehemiah; 1:5; Psalm 11:7, 37:28; Daniel 9:4; Micah 7:18; John 3:16-18; Romans 5;5, 8, 8:28 [Greek text], 38-39; Galatians 2:20; Ephesians 2:4-10, 19, 5:2; 2 Thessalonians 2:16; Titus 3:4-7; 1 John 4:7-11.

1 Corinthians 13:4-8 (NASB) *"*
4 Love is patient,
love is kind and is not jealous;
love does not brag and is not arrogant,
5 does not act unbecomingly;
it does not seek its own (itself),
is not provoked,
does not take into account a wrong suffered,
6 does not rejoice in unrighteousness, but rejoices with the truth;
7 bears all things, believes all things, hopes all things, endures all things.
8 Love never fails;..."

Shrouded In Darkness

Most of the characteristics of love that Paul identifies are easy to understand . The one that presents a problem is the "seek its own." Other translations use words and phrases like: "selfish," "insist on its own way," "its own interests," "demand its own way," "isn't always 'me first'" "self-seeking," and "takes no thought for itself." The word in Greek is simply "own or itself." Everything else is more important, takes priority, never forces or demands first place. Love simply gives without a requirement of love in return.

God is eternal, as stated above in Isaiah 43:10. And is identified as such in Hebrews 13:8 – Jesus is the same yesterday, today, and forever. And in Psalm 102:12, "You, oh God shall endure forever."

One possibly difficult to understand attribute is the Trinity. Jesus identifies this in what many label "The Great Commission," Matthew 28:19 "...make disciples of all peoples, baptizing them in the name of the Father, Son, and Holy Spirit..." The apostle John identifies the trinity in 1 John 4:12-15. The point of difficulty comes with the statement in Deuteronomy 6:4, "...God is One." John 10:30 is where Jesus states that "I and the Father are One." 1 Corinthians 8:4, "...no God but One." And "One God and Father of all..." in Ephesians 4:6. The issue simply stated is, "How can there be three that are one?" It is resolved when the concept of essence is identified – all three are of the same essence, intent, purpose, manner, goals, means; they are always the same in every possible characteristic of personhood and integrity.

God is also merciful and gracious, long-suffering, and abounding in goodness and truth, Exodus 34:6; Psalm 145:17; Romans 3:24, 5:5,20; Hebrews 4:16. Good and upright, Psalm 25:8. Stable and unchanging, James 1:17.

8

God is holy, consecrated and set apart for sacred use only, Exodus 3:5-6; 1 Samuel 2:2; Psalm 99:2-3; Isaiah 6:3; Revelation 4:8.

God is just (justice), He treats everything appropriately according to what or who it is and what its spiritual state of being is (for or against Him, loving or hating Him, etc.), Genesis 8:25; Exodus 34:6-7; Nehemiah 9:32-33; Psalm 99:4; 1 Peter 1:17.

God is omnipotent, has unlimited power, Jeremiah 32:17; Psalm 115:3; Matthew 19:26; Mark 14:36; Romans 11:36; Ephesians 1:11; Hebrews 1:3.

God is omnipresent, everywhere at the same instant of time, 1 Kings 8:27; Job 11:7-9; Jeremiah 23:23-24; Psalm 90:1-2, 139:7-10.

God is omniscient, He knows, and has always known anything about everything, Psalm 147:5; Ezekiel 11:5; Acts 15:18; Romans 2:16, 11:33; 1 John 4:13.

God is righteous, He does the right thing at the right time in the right way, and the end result is the evidence of that righteousness, Genesis 18:25; Psalm 19:7-9, 145:17; Jeremiah 9:24,

There are other characteristics of God that we will discuss shortly. What we have covered is sufficient for us to be able to start making distinctions between Satan and God.

What about the 'modus operandi?'

So far, we've examined the 'bare-bones' data from the Scriptures about the two top generals in the war between good and evil. Having that information is basically good, there is always a need for basic information. The problems with having lots of data, is that there is no inherent sense of how all this data plays out in real life, the day-to-day existence of everything and how, or the way, it is implemented by either general. We need to carefully examine the how and way each general implements all these details.

The How and Way of Satan

There can be a difference between what gets accomplished and the means and mechanism by which it is accomplished. The discussion on the end result will not be done until later, now we will only focus on the how and why, the means and mechanism.

Luke records a discussion that Jesus had with the disciples in chapter 22, verses 25-27. It starts out with "the kings of the Gentiles lord it over them…" In the data on Satan, it identifies that Satan has authority over all the kingdoms of the earth which he used as part of one of the temptations of Jesus. That tells us that the kings of the earth are following Satan's rules, regulations, guidance, etc. The phrase "lord it over" means that they dictate, and exercise power and control over their people.

Acts 10:38 tells us that Jesus healed and delivered all who were oppressed by the devil. The word oppressed means "to exercise power over". In this context the full meaning is that the devil exercises power over people — same as in Luke 22. Satan's basic way of exercising his ways is that of 'lording it over' people. One of the characteristics identifying Satan is the intent to kill steal and destroy. He does this through control of people,

Let's take a look at Jeremiah 25:7,14.

Jeremiah 25:7 (NASB) *"7 Yet you have not listened to Me," declares the Lord, "in order that you might provoke Me to anger with the work of your hands to your own harm."*

Jeremiah 25:14 (NASB) *"14 (For many nations and great kings will make slaves of them, even them; and I will recompense them according to their deeds and according to the work of their hands.)'"*

Here we see that the work of our own hands brings harm to us, and God will reward us according to the work of our hands. The concept of "the work of our hands" simply means that it is an activity that is initiated by our fleshly strength or the ingenuity of our minds. It is unfortunately too easy for Satan to get people to take their own path in life instead of God's way. That in itself will cause God to reward us for those activities and at the same time accomplish Satan's goal to kill, steal and destroy people and God's creation. We wind up doing Satan's work for him at his convincing. This is illustrated in King Ahab's life:

> *2 Chronicles 18:19-21 (NASB) "19 The Lord said, 'Who will entice Ahab king of Israel to go up and fall at Ramoth-gilead?' And one said this while another said that. 20 Then a spirit came forward and stood before the Lord and said, 'I will entice him.' And the Lord said to him, 'How?' 21 He said, 'I will go and be a deceiving spirit in the mouth of all his prophets.' Then He said, 'You are to entice him and prevail also. Go and do so.'"*

At first glance, this may seem like God is actively promoting evil, however, we need to look at the verses from the beginning of the chapter to this point, to understand what is really going on (evaluate the context). We are given what is going on here on earth, and then when Micaiah the Lord's prophet spoke, we find out what all was going on "behind the scenes" in heaven that resulted in the earthly activities. Note that the first time Micaiah spoke he did NOT say that it was from the Lord, he just simply stated to Ahab to go up to Ramoth-gilead and they would succeed. Ahab must have noted this and chastised Micaiah to only tell the truth. Then comes the word that Ahab would fail in verse 16.

Then we come to verse 17 and following which shows us that Ahab had already expected that Micaiah would prophecy failure. And then comes the vision of what had already gone on in heaven. It indicates that God had already declared that Ahab was to be recompensed for his evil deeds. It seems unbelievable that Ahab expected Micaiah to prophecy failure, and after hearing the word from the Lord that a deceiving spirit had given his false prophets a lie, Ahab still wanted to follow the false prophets. This indicates that Ahab was deserving of the lying spirit to his false prophets. It also indicates that Gods word to the lying spirit to succeed was the "seal of the King's signet ring," so to speak, on the judgment of Ahab. Ahab was apparently already predisposed to believe lies instead of the truth. God simply gave Ahab what he wanted. This principle is also reiterated in Romans chapter 1, where Paul states that God turned the unrepentant over to their desires.

The How and Way of God

Continuing the discussion that Jesus had with the disciples in Luke 22, Jesus states that it is not the same way with them (God does not "lord it over" His people [dictate and control]). He then goes on to describe that the way of things in the kingdom of God is the way of a servant. The greatest in God's kingdom is the servant of all, and Jesus comes as a servant. In John 14:9, Jesus says that if you've seen him, you've seen the Father. It should be easy to understand then, that the Father is the greatest servant of all — after all, there is no one greater than God in any form or capacity.

The distinction between Satan's kingdom and God's kingdom is that Satan is the one who controls his kingdom citizens, God relates to His kingdom citizens through being a servant. This 'not controlling' is illustrated in Luke 12:57:

Luke 12:57 (NASB) *"57 And why do you not even on your own initiative judge what is right?"*

I'm going to break this down almost word for word. 'Own': something that is possessed, ownership. 'Initiative': the ability to take action independently. 'Judge': to make a decision (the passing of judgment, sentencing, is not a requirement here). 'Right': most frequently this is translated 'righteous' or 'righteousness', ethical conduct – always doing what is the right thing to do. Using the definitions of the words the statement reads: 'why do you not even on the ability you possess to take action independently, make a decision for what is righteous?' Permit me to rearrange the wording in a way that is common in modern American English: 'You possess the ability to take action independently and make a decision for what is righteous, why are you not doing it?' Over three times in John's Gospel account, Jesus makes a statement to the effect of: 'I say nothing on my own initiative, but only what the Father tells me.' Applying that principal to this verse, Luke 12:57, the situation is that the Father told Jesus to ask that question to the crowd. This statement proves a couple things: 1) People have free choice based on their own initiative, 2) God does not control people (along with the discussion in Luke 22: 25-27). The only 'control' God gives to people, regarding people, is self-control (Galatians 5:22-23). And please, do not forget that God cannot lie (Titus 1:2), so, if God says that we have the ability to take action independently, then that is truth. The concept that 'people possess the ability to take action independently and make a decision for righteousness' is mutually exclusive to the concept of God controlling people. It must be one or the other; it cannot be both.

Satan is the one who controls people, God does not. God uses persuasion to bring people to belief in Jesus for salvation, and the Holy Spirit dwelling within the believer continues to use persuasion to convince them to follow through on God's will and obey His commands (Matthew 28:16-20).

Permit me to digress for a moment to detail what belief and persuasion is from a dictionary definition perspective — we'll get back to God's modus operandi momentarily. Many of our English words are adaptations of words from another language like Latin or Greek or German. Most of the time the words in the two languages (English and the other) mean a very similar thing and are used in a similar manner. There are some words that do have a different connotation, not many, but a few. Faith and believe are in that situation.

In English the word 'faith' depends on the word 'believe', and the word 'believe' depends on the word 'faith'. In informal logic that is classified as a 'circular argument', the premise depends on the conclusion no matter which direction you approach it from. There is no independent third-party word or entity to corroborate (support and confirm) the two words. Many believers think that Hebrews 11:1 is the definition of faith. I would contend that the verse describes how faith works out practically in our day-to-day lives as opposed to being a 'dictionary' definition. You should be able to see that by the time this discussion is finished.

In the Greek language, the word for faith has a root word; English does not have a root word for faith. The Greek root for 'faith' is the word 'persuade'. The Greek meaning of 'faith' is 'to have a firm persuasion'. 'Persuasion' means "the presentation of information, usually with kind words and intentions or motives, to convince someone that something is true'. This excludes the American gangster style of 'persuasion' (one of Satan's means of 'control' of people). God starts with persuasion and continues with it.'

Romans 2:8 provides an interesting viewpoint of persuasion. The key phrasing is "...to those who do not obey the truth but obey unrighteousness,..." Note the use of the word 'obey' twice. The second use is really the word 'persuade', the first use is based on the word 'persuade'. The first use is, in trans-mutilated English, 'apersuade'. In English, we have the words 'typical' and 'atypical'; the usual kind of thing, and the unusual kind of thing. English does not use the word 'persuade' the same way Greek does by placing the letter 'a' at the beginning. The Greek meaning of the first use in this verse is 'to refuse to be persuaded'. Using the meanings of the words instead of 'obey', this verse reads: " "...to those who refuse to be persuaded to the truth but are persuaded to unrighteousness,..." This demonstrates that we can be persuaded to either righteousness or unrighteousness, but note, the process used is persuasion.

This matches up perfectly with John 6:44, 45, 65.

John 6:44, 45, 65 (NASB) *"44 No one can come to Me unless the Father who sent Me draws him; and I will raise him up on the last day.*

45 It is written in the prophets, 'AND THEY SHALL ALL BE TAUGHT OF GOD.' Everyone who has heard and learned from the Father, comes to Me. ...

65 And He was saying, "For this reason I have said to you, that no one can come to Me unless it has been granted him from the Father." "

Let's do another word breakdown First note that all three verses talk about 'come to Jesus'. Verse 44 uses 'draws'. In Greek, this word is written in an aorist-subjunctive form which means that 'draws' is undefined and hypothetical. Please note that most theologians erroneously take this verse as a statement of absolute fact, not hypothetical. The reason Jesus spoke this in an undefined and hypothetical form is because He defined just what He means by the word "draws" in the next verse, 45. The Father provides the teaching and those who hear and learn 'come to Jesus'. Compare the meaning of persuasion with verse 45: 'the presentation of information with kind words and motives' matches up with 'the Father providing the teaching'. 'Hearing and learning' matches up with 'convincing someone of truth'. And the result of that hearing and learning is 'coming to Jesus'. In verse 65, the word 'grants' simply means 'to give'. Verse 45 tells us what the Father gives — teaching, the presentation of information. Our faith is based on, required to have as a foundation, verifiable evidence. Our faith is not a flight of fantasy, it requires evidence.

In Acts 17:2-3, Luke records that when Paul went to a town, he went to the synagogue and "reasoned with them from the Scriptures, explaining and giving evidence that the Christ had to suffer and rise again from the dead," Here we have an example of Paul presenting evidence for those people to base their faith on. Several times Paul stated that we should imitate him as he imitates Christ, and he uses other faithful Christians as examples also. We should do no less - each and every believer has "evidence" of the transformation that has taken place in their own life, and even if one doesn't know all the Bible, their own evidence is their testimony to be shared.

So, we can be persuaded to either righteousness or unrighteousness; the Father provides teaching (the presentation of information with kind words and motives); those who allow themselves to be convinced that the teaching provided by the Father is true, come to Jesus (believe on Him for eternal life); and this is also based on

16

the individual person's ability to take action independently and make a decision for what is righteous (free choice; God does not control people or make their decisions for them). God starts with persuasion and is consistent in using persuasion after the new birth event; God does not control us to come to Jesus, and He does not switch to control afterward, He does not change (Malachi 3:6; James 1:17); God continues the "role" of servant as an example of how we are to be, conformed to the image of His Son, humility etc., all His attributes can only be expressed in love, not control. Love does not "control" the object of that love.

We've now ended our diversion and have arrived back where we left off. Now let's take a look at Jonah and identify an important distinction. Jonah is only 4 chapters long, a short read. The first instance of "control" we find is in Jonah's prayer from the fish, we are told that God commanded the fish and we find out that God command the storm. Later, we find that God controlled the plant, the worm, and the wind. Read the prayers of Jonah carefully. None of the words used indicate that God used any control directly on Jonah. God did not use force, coercion, or anything even near it to make any part of Jonah's body or mind perform or function a certain way, nor did God make Jonah's decisions for him. God obviously can control wind, weather, plants, animals. In the Gospels we read that Jesus cast out demons with a word. The difference we need to be aware of is that plants, animals, weather, etc., are not made in God's image and likeness; same with demons. Jonah is a person made in God's image and likeness. God controls things that are NOT made in His image and likeness.

This last concept is easy to illustrate to make it memorable. It does involve a little bit of simple logic. The logic goes like this: if you have two pieces of information, and if you follow those two pieces of information to their logical conclusion, the information is true. If the logical conclusion is sensible, understandable, and possibly provable through independent validation, then the two pieces of information are true. If the logical conclusion is ridiculous, nonsense, easily proved to be not true, then at least one of the two pieces of information is false. The illustration based on this logic process is: if God created Adam in His own image and likeness, and God created Adam as a controlled being, then God Himself is a controlled being. At that conclusion, one has to ask "Who or what controls God?" That is obviously ludicrous; no one and nothing controls God. Therefore at least one of the two pieces of information is false. We know from Scripture that the first piece is true, it is recorded in the Bible that way — "Let us make man in our own image and likeness..." That is the independent validation of that piece of information. That leaves us with the other piece of information, "If God created Adam as a controlled being," which is false. People are not controlled by God.

Over the more than 58 years I've been a believer, I have heard many times, the phrase: "God is in control." Most of those times, it has turned out to be a derogatory statement blaming God for not answering a prayer or working out a situation the way the person wanted it to be. It was stated in a kindly tone of voice, but was blaming God for what they considered a bad result. There have been a few times I have heard that phrase used as complimentary praise to God, but rarely. That phrase is typically thrown around in conversation without the person consciously understanding what they mean by it.

Let's examine another verse that is badly understood in light of the phrase: "God is in control."

Romans 8:28 (NASB) *"28 And we know that God causes all things to work together for good to those who love God, to those who are called according to His purpose."*

Most modern translations of the Bible are very similar to the NASB. The problem is that the phrase "to those who love God, to those who are called" does not have a "word-for-word" backing in the original Greek. I've studied 4 different books on translation and have not found any discussion on why this verse is translated this way. A simple translation is: "because of the love of God of the called, He works all things together for good according to His purpose." Love is not only the basis for salvation, but is also the basis for God's on-going activities with believers. There is nothing in Paul's description of love which indicates that love controls the object of love. There is an obvious difference between 'love controlling' someone's actions and that someone taking their own initiative based response of love. The distinction is in the source of the action, the controlling one, or the loved one.

Again, Satan is the one who uses control, God uses persuasion and depends on the love response of the one being persuaded. The one being persuaded always has the option to say, "No!" to any of God's requests, there is never any force or coercion involved from God.

Command versus Will

This is another area of theology that has Believers in a quandary pertaining to how God operates. Just about every book on Systematic Theology buries "God's Will" under titles such as "God's Commands and Decrees." There's a real problem with that. Everyone seems to understand that, "commands" are like the General giving orders to the troops – something that absolutely must be obeyed under penalty of something. I took the time to research God's commands throughout the Bible and found that every command God has given pertains to some form of relationship: people to God, people to people, or people to themselves as far as how should they handle their thoughts, emotions, attitudes, and actions toward another being or thing or themselves. Take Jonah for example. God gave Jonah a command to go to Nineveh and preach repentance. That pertains to the relationship between the people of Nineveh and God.

A huge percentage of the commands in the Law pertain to people to people, and people to God; others pertain to people to themselves. Jesus spoke over 70 commands that can be categorized in 49 labels (see my book "*Discipling A New Believer*" by Larry Adams). Every command Jesus gave pertains to the same three general categories of people to God, people to people, people to themselves. These commands are the commands mentioned in Revelation 12 about the 'rest of her offspring who hold to the testimony of Jesus and keep His commands'. And in the Great Commission, 'and teaching them to observe all that I have commanded you'.

The real issue is found in the meaning of the word "will" in the Greek New Testament:

(CWSB Dictionary) "*2307. θέλημα thélēma; gen. thelématos, neut. noun from thélō (G2309), to will. The suffix -ma indicates that it is the result of the will. Will, **not to be conceived as a demand**, but as an expression or inclination of pleasure towards that which is liked, that which pleases and creates joy.*"

This simple definition makes it perfectly clear that, "command" and "will" are totally opposite concepts. A command is a demand, will is not a demand. God's will is simply what would be pleasing to Him, what would make Him happy. A simple example of this is asking a loved one what they want for their birthday. They might rattle off three or four things that would make them happy. Their "list" of things is not a command to go out and

20

buy everything identified. It might be possible that something else that is close or similar to one of the items is purchased and makes that loved one happy. That is just a simple analogy of human relations, please don't take it too far and read extremes into it.

When it comes to God's will, again, it should be based on our love response to Him, and not an act of obedience done just so we don't get smacked. And again, it is based on persuasion.

What is worship?

I have included the dictionary (Lexicon) definitions of the words used in Hebrew, Greek and English that are translated as "worship," at the end of this subsection. Generally speaking, worship is bowing down before a deity. That is an indication of the higher worthiness of the deity, the superior one, and the submission of the one worshipping. Worship is not limited to just singing hymns and praise, it goes deeper than that. There is an aspect of worship which is the word homage, the public display of the honor of the one being worshipped. Giving public display to honor what one worships can take many forms including mimicking the behavior of the one worshipped (like the Elvis impersonators for instance), attesting to the superiority of that one (frequently using verbal phrases of that one and calling its statements and actions great and worthy), and seeking and implementing the goals of that one.

We have an old adage: "Imitation is the sincerest form of flattery." The earliest known use of this exact expression is in Charles Caleb Colton's 1820 *Lacon: or Many Things in Few Words, addressed to those who think.* But there are earlier variations such as a 1714 issue of *The Spectator* magazine which included the phrase: Imitation is a kind of artless flattery. (bookbrowse.com)

Paul (and others) discuss imitation of himself, Christ, God several times: 1 Corinthians 4:16, 11:1; Ephesians 5:1; 1 Thessalonians 1:6, 2:14; Hebrews 6:12, 13:7; 3 John 1:11. It seems that the New Testament concept is "imitation is the sincerest form of worship." That can have devastating consequences.

If we are to imitate Paul, Christ, God, good Christians, as a form of worship of God, is it possible that if someone imitates characteristics, mannerisms and end results of Satan, that they are worshiping Satan? I'll bet you never thought of it that way… People will only imitate someone or something they believe is worthy of their effort. If they don't believe it, they won't imitate it, unless they are mocking it (which is usually obvious). So, when people imitate Satan's methods, means, and achieve his desired results, they are worshipping Satan, whether they believe in a spiritual world view or not.

Worship: (CWSB Dictionary) H7812. שָׁחָה shāchāh: A verb meaning to bow down, to prostrate oneself, to crouch, to fall down, to humbly beseech, to do reverence, to worship. The primary meaning of the word is to bow down. This verb is used to indicate bowing before a monarch or a superior and paying homage to him or her (Gen. 43:28).

Worship: (CWSB Dictionary) 4352. προσκυνέω proskunéō; contracted proskunó, fut. proskunḗsō, from prós (G4314), to, and kunéō (n.f.), to kiss, adore. To worship, do obeisance, show respect, fall or prostrate before. Literally, to kiss toward someone, to throw a kiss in token of respect or homage. The ancient oriental (especially Persian) mode of salutation between persons of equal ranks was to kiss each other on the lips; when the difference of rank was slight, they kissed each other on the cheek; when one was much inferior, he fell upon his knees and touched his forehead to the ground or prostrated himself, throwing kisses at the same time toward the superior. It is this latter mode of salutation that Gr. writers express by proskunéō. In the NT, generally, to do reverence or homage to someone, usually by kneeling or prostrating oneself before him. In the Sept.

it means to bow down, to prostrate oneself in reverence, homage (Gen. 19:1; 48:12).

Worship: (CWSB Dictionary) 4576. σέβομαι sébomai; fut. sebésomai, pass. deponent. to worship. To worship, to reverence. In the NT, only in the mid. (Matt. 15:9; Mark 7:7 quoted from Is. 29:13; Acts 16:14; 18:7, 13; 19:27; Sept.: Josh. 4:24; Job 1:9). The part. noun sebómenos, a worshiper of the true God (Acts 13:43, 50; 16:14; 17:4, 17). These were Gentile proselytes as expressed in Acts 13:43.

Worship: (CWSB Dictionary) 2356. θρησκεία thrēskeía; gen. thrēskeías, fem. noun from thrēskeúō (n.f.), to worship God, which is from thréskos (G2357), religious, pious. Worshiping or worship. In Col. 2:18, mentions the worship of angels. This is probably a gen. of association and alludes to the false, gnostic doctrine of celestial exaltation in which human worshipers were permitted to share in the worship activities of various grades of angelic beings. It also refers to the true worship of God (Acts 26:5; James 1:26, 27). Thrēskeía is contrasted with theosébeia (G2317), external worship, meaning reverential worship, and eusébeia (G2150), piety or godliness, and eulábeia (G2124), devotion arising from godly fear or acceptance of what God directs or permits. Thrēskeía may thus refer only to ceremonial service or worship as Paul refers to the religion of the Jews (Acts 26:5). James refers to pure religion (James 1:26, 27), indicating there is also an impure religion which would be external worship but not the practice of that which God demands of man.

Worship: wor·ship| ˈwərSHəp | nounthe feeling or expression of reverence and adoration for a deity: the worship of God | ancestor worship.
• the acts or rites that make up a formal expression of reverence for a deity; a religious ceremony or ceremonies: the church was opened for public worship.

24

• *adoration or devotion comparable to religious homage, shown toward a person or principle: our society's worship of teenagers.* • *archaic honor given to someone in recognition of their merit.* • *[as title] (His/ Your Worship) mainly British used in addressing or referring to an important or high-ranking person, especially a magistrate or mayor: we were soon joined by His Worship the Mayor. verb (worships, worshiping, worshiped; also worships , worshipping, worshipped) [with object] show reverence and adoration for (a deity); honor with religious rites: the Maya built jungle pyramids to worship their gods.* • *[no object] take part in a religious ceremony: he went to the cathedral because he chose to worship in a spiritually inspiring building.* • *treat (someone or something) with the reverence and adoration appropriate to a deity: she adores her sons and they worship her.*

Homage: *hom·age| ˈ(h)ämij | noun special honor or respect shown publicly: they paid homage to the local boy who became president | a masterly work written in homage to Beethoven.*

Wisdom: The appropriate application of knowledge

John 16:13-14 (NASB) "*13 But when He, the Spirit of truth, comes, He will <u>guide</u> you into all the truth; for He will not speak on His own initiative, but <u>whatever He hears, He will speak</u>; and He will <u>disclose</u> to you what is to come. 14 He will glorify Me, for He will take of Mine and will <u>disclose</u> it to you.*"

John 10:27 (NASB) "*27 My sheep <u>hear My voice</u>, and I know them, and they follow Me;*"

1 Kings 19:12 (NASB) "*12 After the earthquake a fire, but the LORD was not in the fire; and after the fire a sound of a <u>gentle blowing</u>.*"

Guide: (CWSB Dictionary) "*3594. ὁδηγέω hodēgéō; contracted hodēgṓ, fut. hodēgḗsō, from hodēgós (G3595), guide, leader. To lead the way, guide*"

Disclose: (CWSB Dictionary) "*312. ἀναγγέλλω anaggéllō; fut. anaggelṓ, aor. anéggeila, 2d aor. pass. anēggélēn, from aná (G0303), on, upon, and aggéllō (n.f., see below), to tell, declare, which is from ággelos (G0032), messenger. To announce, make known, declare, tell of things done*"

Gentle: (CWSB Dictionary) "*H1851. דַּק daq: An adjective meaning gaunt, fine, thin; dwarfish; low. It indicates that something is weak, undernourished, fine, small*"

Blowing: (CWSB Dictionary) "*H1827. דְּמָמָה demāmāh: A feminine noun indicating hushed, a whisper. It indicates a soft gentle blowing or whisper in contrast to the roar of an earthquake, fire, or a storm at sea*"

Listening to the "small whisper" of the Holy spirit can never be underestimated, in spite of how often that happens in the conversations of Christians. If you carefully read through Isaiah and Jeremiah, one of the things that stand out is the repeated frequency of God identifying that the Israelites failed to listen to His voice. Deuteronomy chapter 28 discusses the blessings and the curses involved in either listening or not listening to the VOICE of the Lord; it uses more than three times as many words to describe the curses for not listening as it does to the blessings of listening. Listening to the voice of the Lord is a consistent theme throughout the entire Bible. It seems as though the Church today has largely lost the ability to listen to His voice. The wisdom, teaching, guidance and all the characteristics that Jesus refers to in John chapters 14 through 16 only comes to us through the "small whisper" of the Holy Spirit. Listening to the "small whisper" of the Lord, the Holy Spirit, is just as important today as it was back in the time of the Books of Genesis to Nehemiah. God does not change. Just as God took walks with Adam and Eve in the cool of the day in the Garden of Eden, it seems obvious that they must have had discussions, and that is still part of what God wants in a relationship with people today. God's wisdom must come to us through His "small whisper."

God's written word, the Bible, contains the principles and concepts that we need to know regarding salvation, righteousness and every aspect of our relation to God and each other in salvation. It is through His "small whisper" that we find the wisdom to be able to apply these principles and concepts in any specific situation. We will always be dependent on God for everything we say and do. When someone feels called to become a pastor or missionary, they are listening to that "small whisper."

When we follow the leading of that "small whisper" in regard to the details of the generals of both sides of the spiritual war between good and evil, we will find the source of turmoil in the world. We must take God's wisdom for applying all the details of both sides of the conflict and not try to use the ingenuity of our fleshly minds to figure everything out. If we do something in the strength of the flesh, or the ingenuity of our minds, we are doing things the way Satan wants us to do it - effectively worshipping him, not God; and bringing harm and destruction to ourselves.

Putting it all together

We have identified that Satan exists, and is actively promoting his war against God and mankind. The characteristics of Satan, his methods, means, goals have been contrasted against God's ways. This is going to sound insanely simplistic, but, it really is. With all this information about the war between good and evil, it should be easy to figure out what and who is behind turmoil. If the process or end result contains any of the characteristics of Satan that have been identified from the Bible, then whatever, or whoever, it is, is worshipping Satan. This is true even if that whoever does not believe in anything spiritual. Gravity exists and functions even if you don't believe in it — the spiritual realm exists and has it's influence on everyone and everything even if someone does not believe it. Let me repeat for emphasis: if the process or result has any lying, deceit, killing, or any other characteristic of Satan's means, methods, or goals, it is Satan worship. Those who practice Satan worship will pay their own ultimate price themselves — eternal death, separation from the God of life. We only have two sources of spiritual information, Satan or God. When we imitate one or the other, that is all that is necessary to worship that one, whichever that may be.

The mouth speaks out of that which fills the heart (Matthew 12:34; Proverbs 4:23; Proverbs 10:11; Psalm 14:1; Proverbs 21:2; Proverbs 24:12; Ezekiel 11:21; Ezekiel 16:30; Luke 6:45). We speak either godly or satanically, there is no middle ground.

Being "politically correct" is effectively calling something by a label that does not necessarily provide anything accurate about the item. I have a hard time making any distinction between being "politically correct" and being a liar. It seems that most of Christianity today wants to be "politically correct" so no one "gets offended."

I've already identified that we (Christians) should be imitating Christ, God, etc., but have you considered that God Himself took no concern about calling sin for the sin it is in Isaiah, Jeremiah, and all the 'minor' prophets? Jesus, in the Gospels, had no problem in identifying the sins of the religious hierarchy of His day. When Christians are being "politically correct" are they no longer imitating God? (1 Peter 2:1; 1 Timothy 5:15) That does not give anyone privilege to be nasty about it, but we need to be politely accurate, truthful, righteous, about good versus evil, truth versus lies, righteousness versus unrighteousness, and all those other possible aspects of the war we are in. This is a critical point which requires each and every Christian to be listening to the "small whisper" of the Holy Spirit within us for the wisdom for being politely truthful in everything we say. I have a suspicion that the old "hell fire and brimstone" preachers might have chased more people away from God than were attracted to salvation.

The most frequently repeated sin that God identified in the prophets was the failure to listen to God's VOICE. And they had to do that without the indwelling of the Holy Spirit. Unfortunately, we could rewrite Isaiah, Jeremiah, and the others with words identifying the Church in stead of Israel, and it would be just as true today as it was back in the Old Testament times. God did not get laryngitis when the Church was born, Jesus still expects us to listen to His VOICE. How much easier it should be for believers to listen to the "small whisper" of the Holy Spirit with Him dwelling within us. God is not going to lead us into anything where He cannot sustain us with His word and strength — that's called walking by faith.

We only have two choices, Satan worship, or God worship. If we are not doing one, then we are doing the other, there is no middle ground, either we are partaking of demons or the Lord (1 Corinthians 10:21). We are either for Christ or against Him (Matthew 12:30; Mark 9:;40; Luke 9:50, 11:23) - Jesus never gave us any middle ground, or shades of grey on this.

As Shakespeare said, "All the world's a stage," and Satan is currently the staring actor until Christ returns. The Church (meaning each and every believer) needs to be shining their light of life into the shroud of darkness that hides the activity of the evil one from the eyes and minds of those who worship him.

God's Battle Instructions

Ephesians 6:10-18 (NASB) "*10 Finally, be strong in the Lord and in the strength of His might. 11 Put on the full armor of God, so that you will be able to stand firm against the schemes of the devil. 12 For our struggle is not against flesh and blood, but against the rulers, against the powers, against the world forces of this darkness, against the spiritual forces of wickedness in the heavenly places. 13 Therefore, take up the full armor of God, so that you will be able to resist in the evil day, and having done everything, to stand firm. 14 Stand firm therefore, HAVING GIRDED YOUR LOINS WITH TRUTH, and HAVING PUT ON THE BREASTPLATE OF RIGHTEOUSNESS, 15 and having shod YOUR FEET WITH THE PREPARATION OF THE GOSPEL OF PEACE; 16 in addition to all, taking up the shield of faith with which you will be able to extinguish all the flaming arrows of the evil one. 17 And take THE HELMET OF SALVATION, and the sword of the Spirit, which is the word of God.*

18 With all prayer and petition pray at all times in the Spirit, and with this in view, be on the alert with all perseverance and petition for all the saints,"

2 Corinthians 10:3-5 *"... our weapons not of flesh, but divinely powerful to pull down strongholds...."*

There have been a lot of ideas thrown about regarding the practical application of the full armor of God. Many think there are only six pieces to it, but the Scripture lists seven(7). For some reason praying in the Spirit gets reduced to just simple prayer, and is not considered by most theologians as part of God's armor. Let me provide an example to identify the importance of praying in the Spirit. Imagine a country that develops the greatest army and weaponry the world has ever imagined. However, that country fails to provide the means and mechanisms of getting their army to the battlefield and sustaining it there. What good would their army really be??? It would be less than useless. The same applies to Paul's description of the full armor of God here in Ephesians. The armor is less than useless if we cannot get to the battlefield. That means praying in the Spirit is the seventh part of the full armor of God. Maybe the problem with a lot of theologians is that they have a form that looks godly, but denies the power of God through praying in the Spirit. There really is power in prayer led, guided, and facilitated through the Holy Spirit.

Satan will design his schemes to interfere with or prohibit your use of what God has given you. We fight through *praying in the Spirit*. That means we stand before God on His throne on the basis of the Gospel of Peace (*shoes*, peace with God that was made by the sacrifice of Jesus on the cross and His resurrection), a heart intent to pursue righteousness (*breastplate*), based on the truth of God's Word (*belt*), the transformation of our minds by the work of the Holy Spirit (*helmet*), having a firm resolution and persuasion in our hearts and minds that God is for us and that faith will overcome everything the enemy throws at us (*shield of faith*), and knowing God's word, the Bible (*the sword of the Spirit*), and being able to listen to the still small whisper voice of the Lord for what can be applied from the Bible to any specific situation (scheme, attack of the enemy), and being able to speak that truth into the situation – All these items being used in prayer in the Spirit, knowing that the war is in the "second heaven", and we are before the throne in the "third heaven", simply requesting that the victory in Christ at the cross and His resurrection be applied to the situation at hand.

We obtain the victory through *praying in the Spirit* and then speak that victory into the situation according to God's wisdom, not the strength of the flesh or the ingenuity of our own minds.

Appendix A "What the Believer needs to overcome the enemy and be what God intended."

1. Rom. 1-8, Salvation
2. Rom. 12-16, Life/walk of/by faith
3. Eph. 1-3, Believer's position
4. Eph. 4-6, Believer's heavenly walk
5. Jn. 16:8-11, The Comforter beside us Jn. 1:12, 13; Jn. 3:5-8; Gal. 6:15; Titus 3:5; 2 Cor. 5:17; 2 Pet. 1:4; Col. 1:13; Gal. 1:4; Rom. 8:9; Col. 1:27; Gal. 2:20; 2 Cor. 13:5; Rom. 5:5; 1 Cor. 2:12; 1 Cor. 6:19; Phil. 3:20; 2 Cor. 5:1-8 (Heb. 3:1; Eph. 2:6. See also Mt. 18:35; Jn. 3:12; 1 Cor. 15:48. Heavenly standing)
6. The Christian is 'heavenly'
-by calling (Heb. 3:1),
-by citizenship (Phil. 3:20),
-by inheritance (1 Pet. 1:4) and
-by resurrection life (Eph. 2:6),
-as a member of that body of which the Head is actually in heaven. The heavenly (or 'in heavenly places,') therefore, is the sphere of the believer's present association with Christ. This is shown by the constant context, 'in Christ Jesus.'
7. The believer is now associated with Christ in
-life (Col. 3:4; 1 Jn. 5:11, 12),
-position (Eph. 2:6),
-suffering (Rom. 8:18; 2 Tim. 2:11, 12; Col. 1:24; Phil. 1:29);
-service, (Jn. 17:18; Mt. 28:18-20), and
-betrothal (2 Cor. 11:1-3).
8. The believer is to be associated with Christ in
-Glory (Jn. 17:22; Rom. 8:18; Col. 3:4),

-inheritance (Rom. 8:17),
-authority (Mt. 19:28; Rev. 3:21), and
-marriage (Eph. 5:22, 33; Rev. 19:1-9).
9. The believer's 'spiritual blessings' (Eph. 1:3), therefore, are to be possessed or experienced only as he lives in the sphere of his joint life, joint position, joint suffering, joint service and joint marriage pledge with Christ. In so far as he lives as a natural man whose interests are earthly, and avoids the path of co-service and (if need be) co-suffering, he will know nothing experimentally of the exalted blessings of Ephesians. 'It is sufficient that the servant be as his Master.' [Mat. 10:25] Christ took account of Himself as a heavenly Being come down to earth to do His Father's will." (Scofield Bible Correspondence Course, Book 2; page 288.)

Appendix B: Finding the love of God for eternal life

Back on page 10 the verses in Jeremiah 25:7, 14 were identified. These indicate that when we do things in our own strength or the ingenuity of our minds, we bring ourselves harm and God will fully repay people for their works. 1 Peter 3:16 tells us that we can twist the Scriptures to our own destruction. Romans 5:19 shows that through the sin of Adam we all became sinners, incapable of hitting the mark or reaching the goal. Everyone is a sinner is specified in Romans 3:23. We cannot achieve what God intended people to be in our own strength. God has given us self-control, however, before a person believes on Jesus, they can only control themselves in their own strength which will only result in harm and getting what they deserve. Romans chapter 1 tells us that God will give us what we desire, no matter what those consequences might be. Love does not control others. One of the differences between an unbeliever and a believer is that the believer has access to "The Designer's Instruction Guide," the Holy Spirit dwelling within the believer who can teach and guide the believer in using self-control so that harm and destruction could be avoided.

John 3:16-18 (NASB) [16] *"For God so loved the world, that He gave His only begotten Son, that whoever believes in Him shall not perish, but have eternal life.* [17] *For God did not send the Son into the world to judge the world, but that the world might be saved through Him.* [18] *He who believes in Him is not judged; he who does not believe has been judged already, because he has not believed in the name of the only begotten Son of God."*

The key is believing in Jesus. The details of that belief are:

Jesus is the Son of God, born into humanity through a virgin. Matthew 1:18-25; Luke 1:26-38.

Jesus lived a sinless life, meaning He never sinned. John 19:4; 2 Corinthians 5:21; Hebrews 4:15; 1 Peter 2:22; 1 John 3:5.

Jesus voluntarily died on the cross, shed His blood to fulfill the required penalty for sin, death, which each one would otherwise have to pay themselves. Every person ever born or ever will be born, except Jesus, is a sinner desiring sin instead of righteousness. The wages of sin is death, but the free gift of God is eternal life and forgiveness of our sins, all because Jesus paid the cost. John 10:17-18.

Jesus was buried in a tomb.Matthew 27:57-61; John 19:38-42.

Jesus was raised by God on the third day. Matthew 28:1-20.

Jesus was seen after His resurrection one time by over 500 people, and spent many days explaining to His disciples about Himself from the Bible. 1 Corinthians 15:1-11; Luke 24:27, 45-48.

Jesus ascended into heaven 40 days after rising from death where He awaits God the Father's timing for His second coming. Luke 24:50-53; Acts 1:9-11.

Believing on Jesus is an everything-or-nothing situation. There is no such thing as being partly saved. God requires all of our being. Believing on Jesus for salvation, eternal life, requires the repentance of the one seeking the salvation. Repentance is simply a change of mind, and then one believes in their heart. Mark 1:15; Luke 24:47; Acts 3:19; 20:21.

When you consider all these facts to be true (repent - a change of mind) and believe (have a firm persuasion [faith] in) in your heart that they are true, the Holy

Spirit will come and live inside you, in your spirit and will teach and guide you into all the truth. You must continually follow through on working out God's truth in your life. He will supply you with His wisdom and strength to stay true to all the principles and concepts of godliness in the Bible.

Tell someone what you believe - everyone speaks what is on their heart, the things they truly believe. Romans 10:9-10; 1 Samuel 24:13; Isaiah 32:6; Matthew 12:34, 35; 15:18; Luke 6:45; Ephesians 4:29; James 3:2-12.

Back on page 13, Luke 12:57 was broken down to understand the words used. This statement of Jesus tells us that each person has the ability to take action independently and make a decision for what is righteous. Each person must make that decision for themselves, no person can make that decision for another person. Faith is an individual, personal thing.

A comment about the word "faith." In Greek, faith is in the passive voice which means that faith does not initiate action in and of itself. Faith is a state of being, expecting to be acted upon from something outside itself. This fits with the fact that we can do nothing to earn or deserve salvation, eternal life from God, it is His work, not ours. When we believe, we are then in the state of being which allows the Holy Spirit to come and dwell within our spirit so that the relationship with God can begin.